Golf
MANIA

Cartoons by Qwisi

RAVETTE BOOKS

This edition published by
Ravette Books Limited
© Ravette Books Limited 1985
Reprinted 1986, 1987 (twice), 1988,
1989 (three times), 1992, 1994

First published by
A/S Interpresse, Box 11, 2880 Bagsvaerd,
Copenhagen, Denmark,
© Hans Qvist of A/S Interpresse, 1983

Printed and bound in Great Britain
for Ravette Books Limited,
25/31 Tavistock Place
London WC1H 9SU
An Egmont Company
by Cox & Wyman Ltd.
Reading

Editor: Nigel Foster

ISBN: 1 85304 771 6

'But the 7th hole, now that was something else. Daddy hit a *fabulous* drive, it took an unlucky bounce and ended up behind a tree. But then I took my 5 iron and . . .'

'How many points for hitting your
ball into that charming little lake, dear?'

'Fascinating game, golf. You see,
if your drive is even a *little* bit out . . .'

'Taking into account the seven kids,
it's been one hell of a good investment.'

6

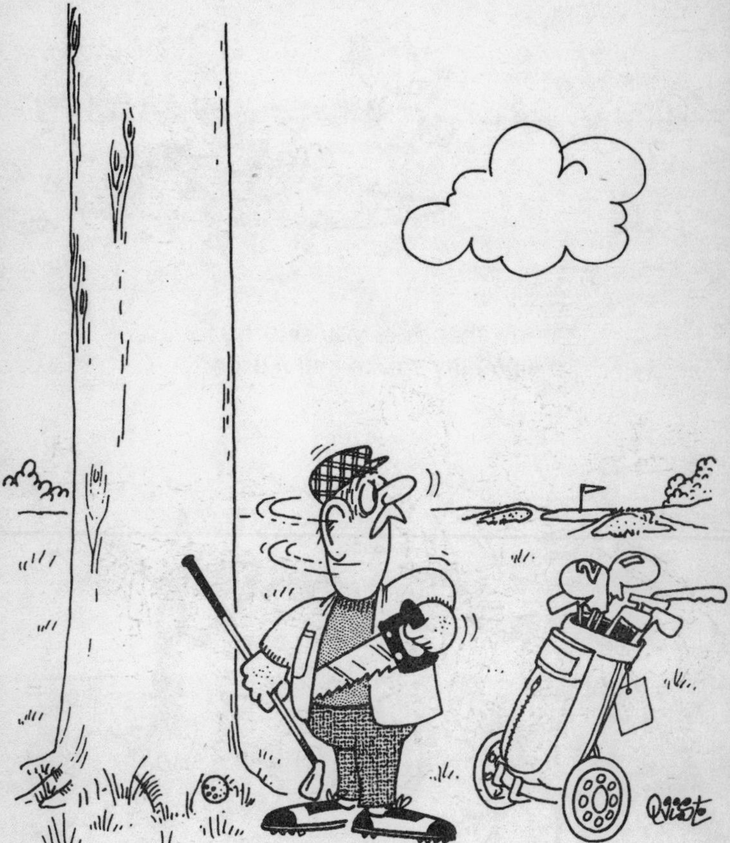

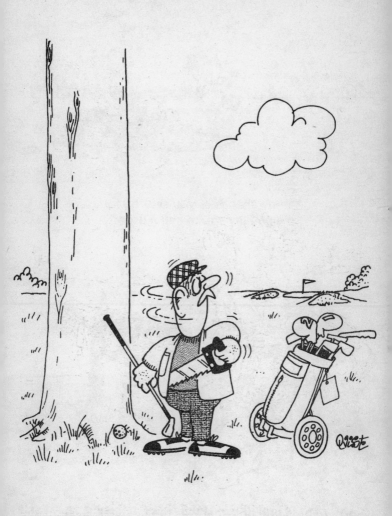

'Any chance of you settling for
a penalty stroke and a drop?'

'Sorry to hold you up – that was the hospital. It seems the
wife's given birth to a couple of something-or-others.'

'Next year's Masters, Faldo about to eagle
the thirteenth and the horizontal hold went!'

'Lucky I grabbed it, mate, or you *might*
have lost your ball down that little hole.'

'Sometimes I wonder if John really
has given up snooker for golf.'

'You'll just have to accept it, Mr Higgins – some people
do have a natural slice. But that doesn't necessarily
make you a bad person.'

'For the last time, Miles – when your father comes
home early, never ask him how well he played!'

'Honestly, Charles – this isn't what I expected when you promised to spend less time on the golf course!'

'Chap who sold it to me said it would teach me
to keep my head still once and for all.'

14

And please send me a driver and a crate of balls.

'How long have you been with the firm, Jones?'

'Can't you forget that slice of yours
for even a moment, Edwin?'

'When for once you do the washing-up, darling,
I wish you'd do it with good grace.'

'Given he was caught falsifying his score card,
it was bad form to wear the club tie to the very last.'

'What you seem to need, Mr Higgins, is some
work to take your mind off your hobby.'

'Yes, I've seen six or seven of those already.
I wonder if they're part of some kind of drainage?'

'Shouldn't we forget about the ball, Sir,
and try and find the course?'

'If you're goin' out golfing today, she said,
it'll be over my dead body.'

'Well, that's one sort of club record:
two and a half twists and a lost ball!'

'Yes, yes, yes. But your ulcer will have to wait
until I've heard the results of the Open.'

'When you find the rule that says it's not permitted,
I'll take it off and not before.'

'Okay – how about an advance on two years'
pocket money if Dad borrows it for an hour or so?'

'I heard he actually *began* his round in the Summer.'

'Oh blast! Three inches out again.'

'Relax. This isn't going to take long . . .'

'Have I or haven't I stayed at home to
help you in the garden – yes or no?'

'The doctor says I should tell you the truth – and to begin with, your putting's a disaster.'

'Hurry up, Bill. There's no queue up at the 1st tee at all.'

'Excuse me. Are all the bunkers
on this course as bad as this one?'

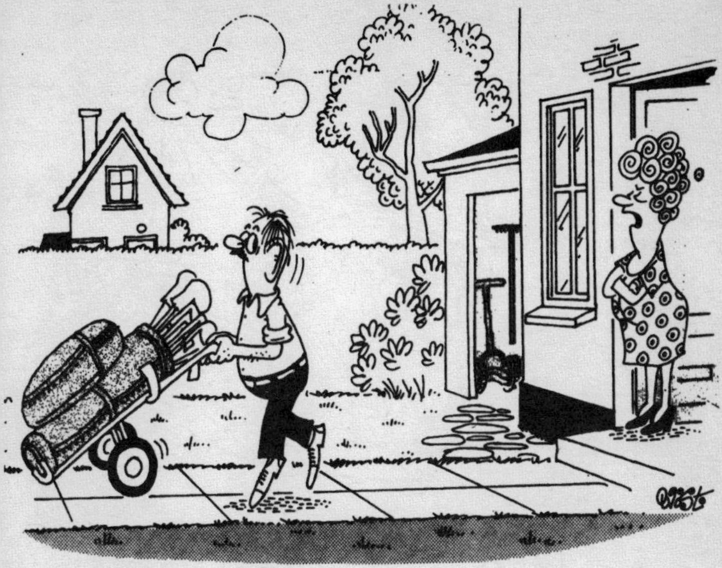

'Wrong again, Edwin. That's not the lawn-mower.'

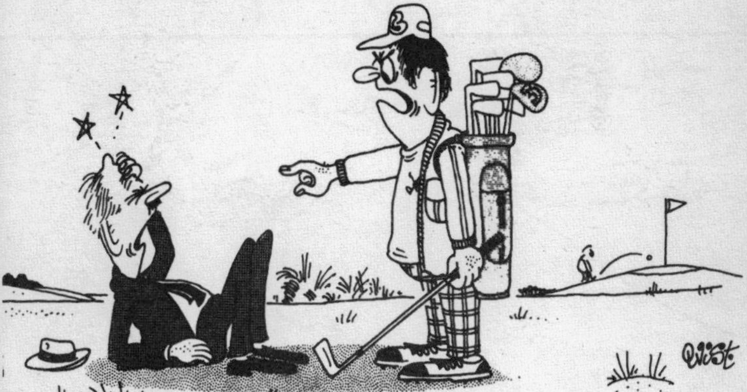

'Oh, stop snivelling. What's happened to my ball?'

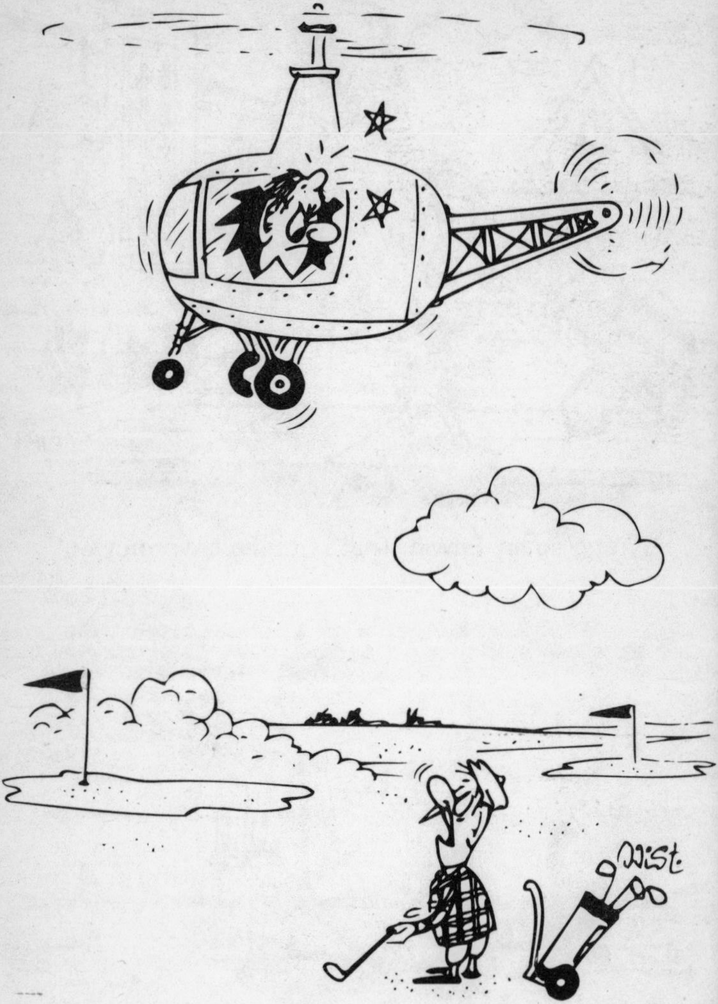
Wist

'I said I'm sorry.'

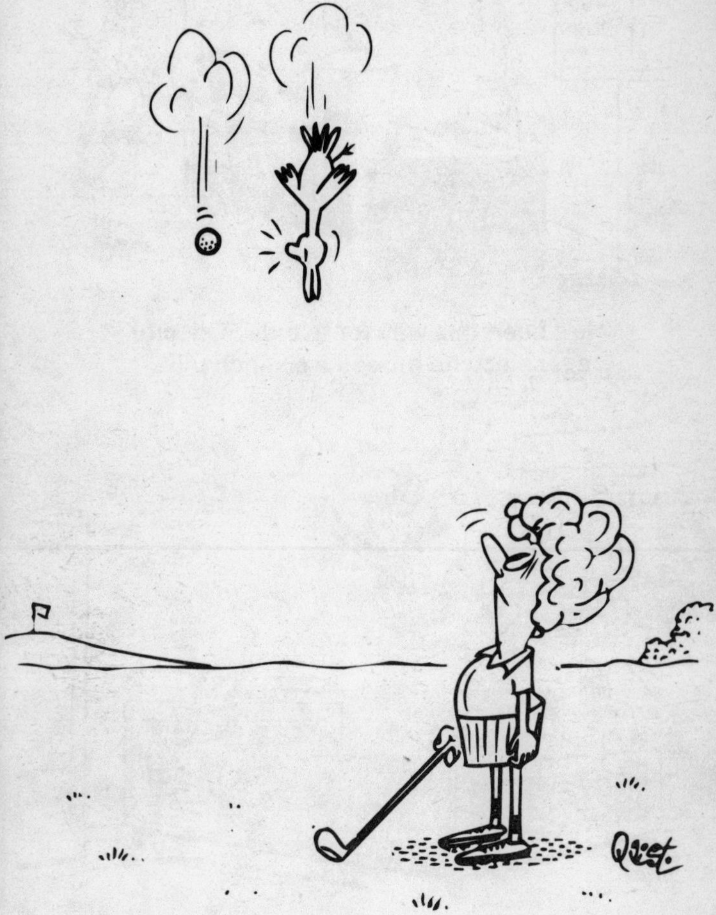
Quist

'He's been this way for two days, doctor,
ever since he missed a six-inch putt.'

'Let me guess – it's the day of the
Old Boys' Reunion golf match, right?'

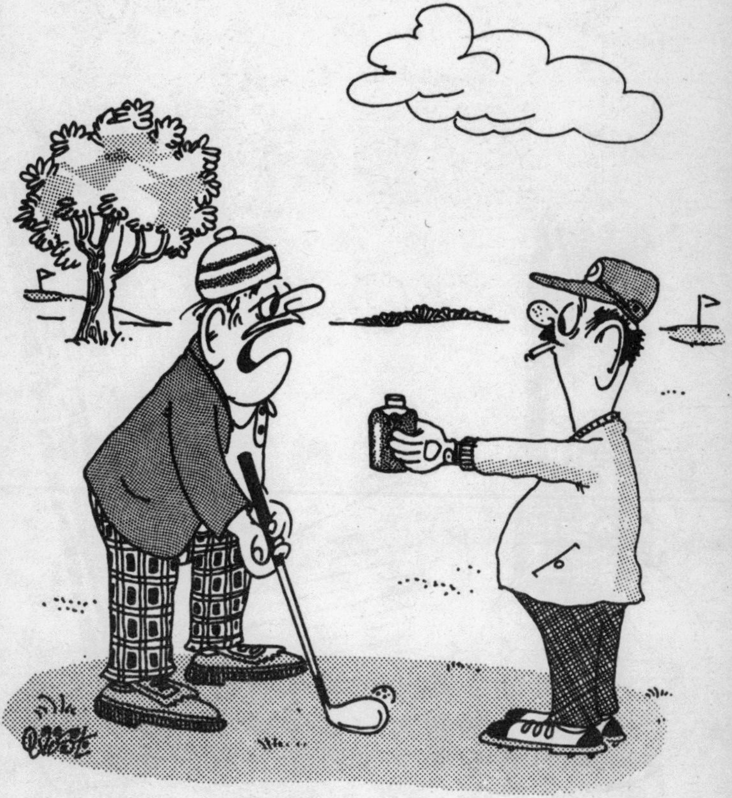

'No thanks – I'm driving.'

'Well so far there's been no sign of life . . .'

'I've never been able to work out whether
he's overworked, plain lazy or out golfing.'

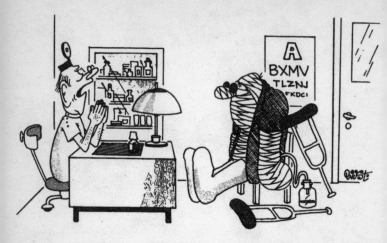

'Yes, quite. But what about your golf?'

'Experience tells me, we'd better get to bed.'

38

'This is certainly the toughest course I've yet seen.'

'Personally, I love the fact that
I can park absolutely anywhere.'

'Well . . . at least the direction was right, dear.'

'And I'd advise you not to play more than
27 holes a day for the next couple of weeks.'

'Oh those – I don't really know, but I *think*
George won them at some sort of game.'

'Whoever he is, I don't fancy playing against him.'

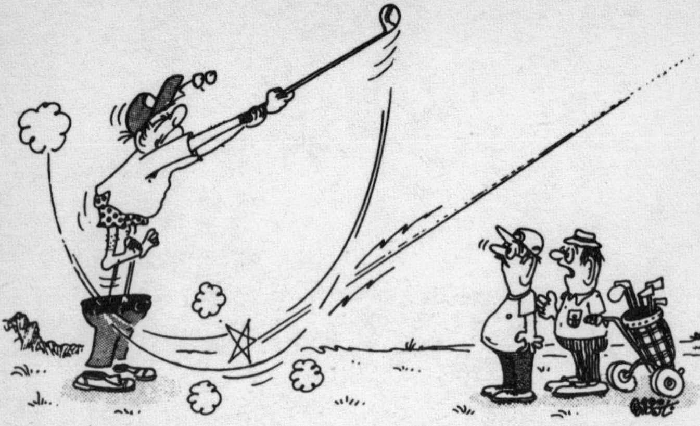

'Well, perhaps not the most *elegant* style – but still the hardest hitter in the club.'

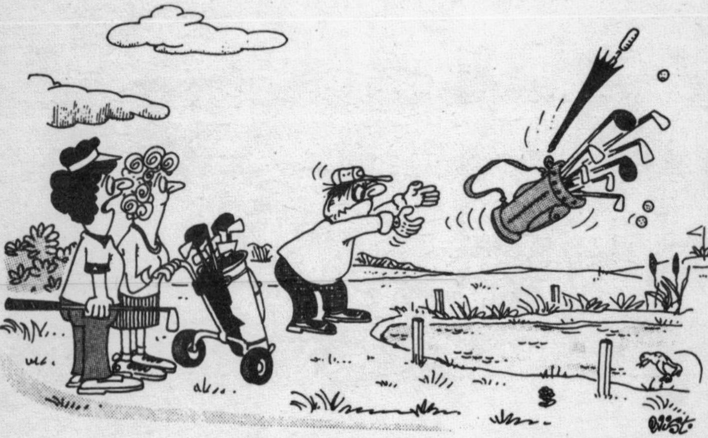

'Actually, we saved more money when Tom spent all his spare time in bars and nightclubs.'

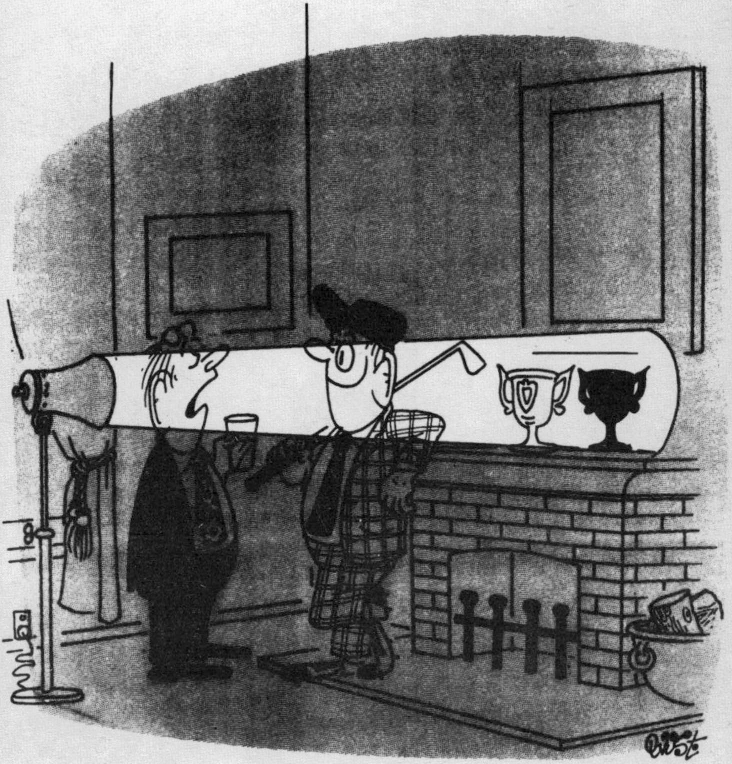

'So, what's new?'

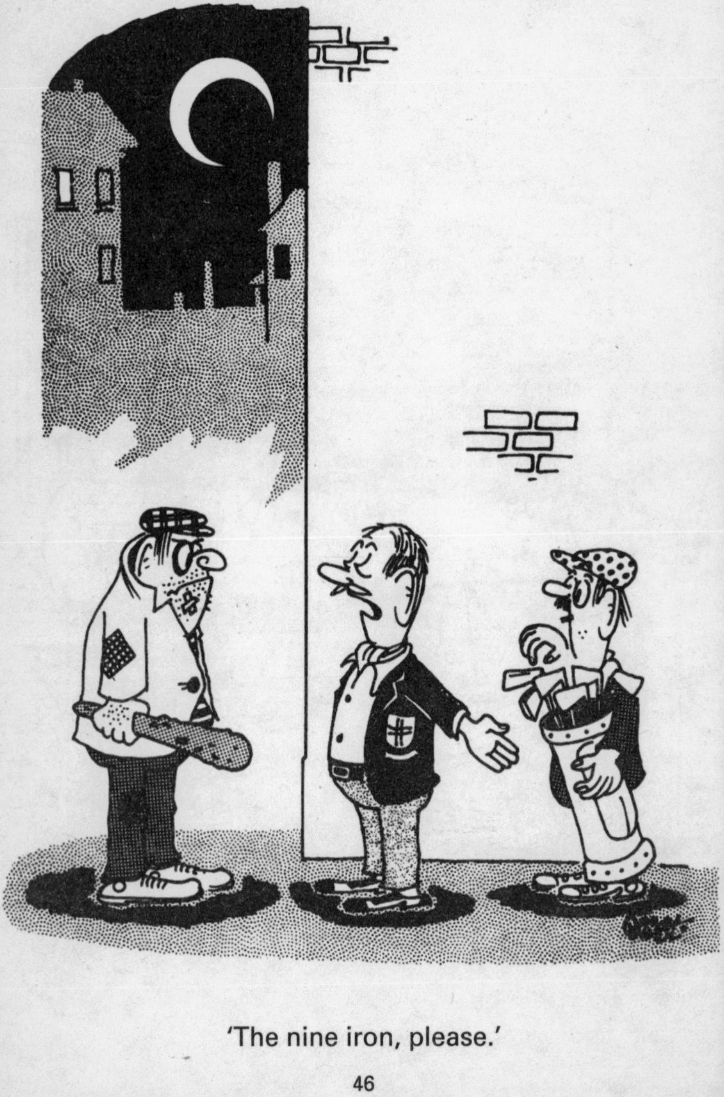

'The nine iron, please.'

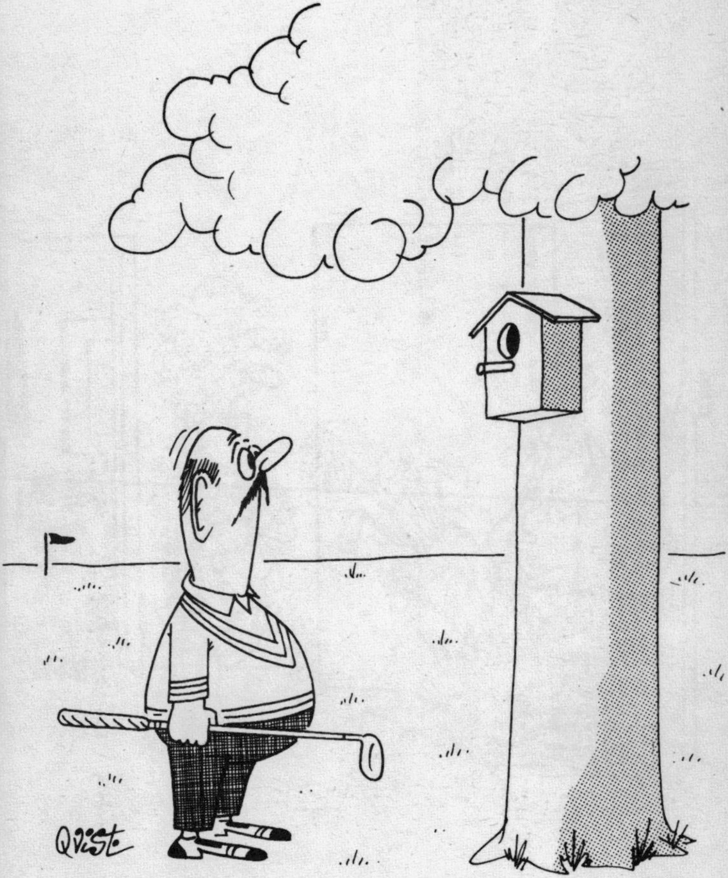
QVISTE

'Are you trying to tell me you've had
a hole-in-one again, Herbert?'

'I think of it as a slow but necessary re-adjustment
after a three-week golfing holiday.'

'This, I think, has got to be the limit.'

'Remember, dear – a firm, steady grip and a
smooth shoulder movement gives you that
desirable, rhythmic stroke.'

'Sorry I'm late, boys. They added another
psalm after the ceremony.'

'It's my biography, called "How I Quit Business
And Took Up Golf For Fun And Profit."'

'I don't know what it is he's invented,
but he's never at home any more.'

'No, the General Manager went out about twenty minutes ago, but I'm expecting him back any minute!'

'Gee, Howard, it's ages since you put your arms around me like that.'

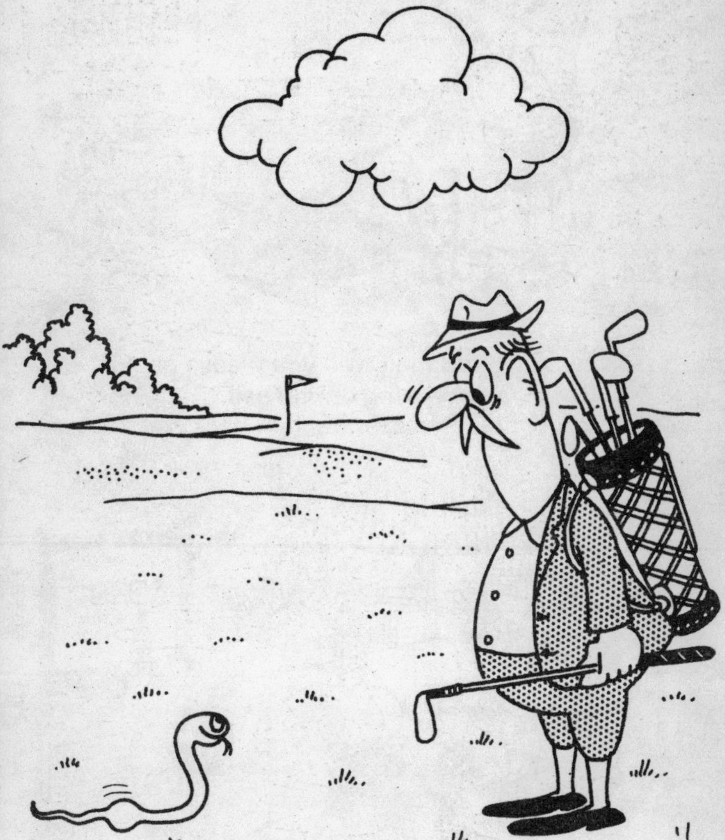
QUIST

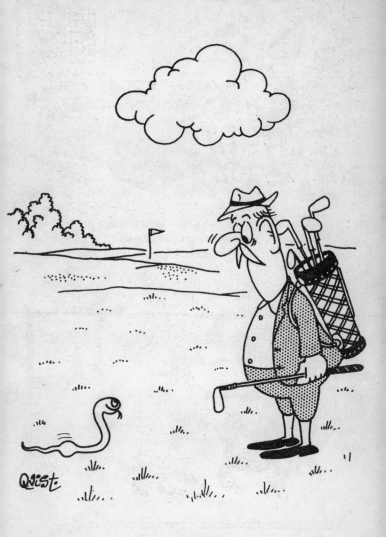

'Now, my good man, will you please get up.
You're lying on my ball.'

'HERBERT...!'

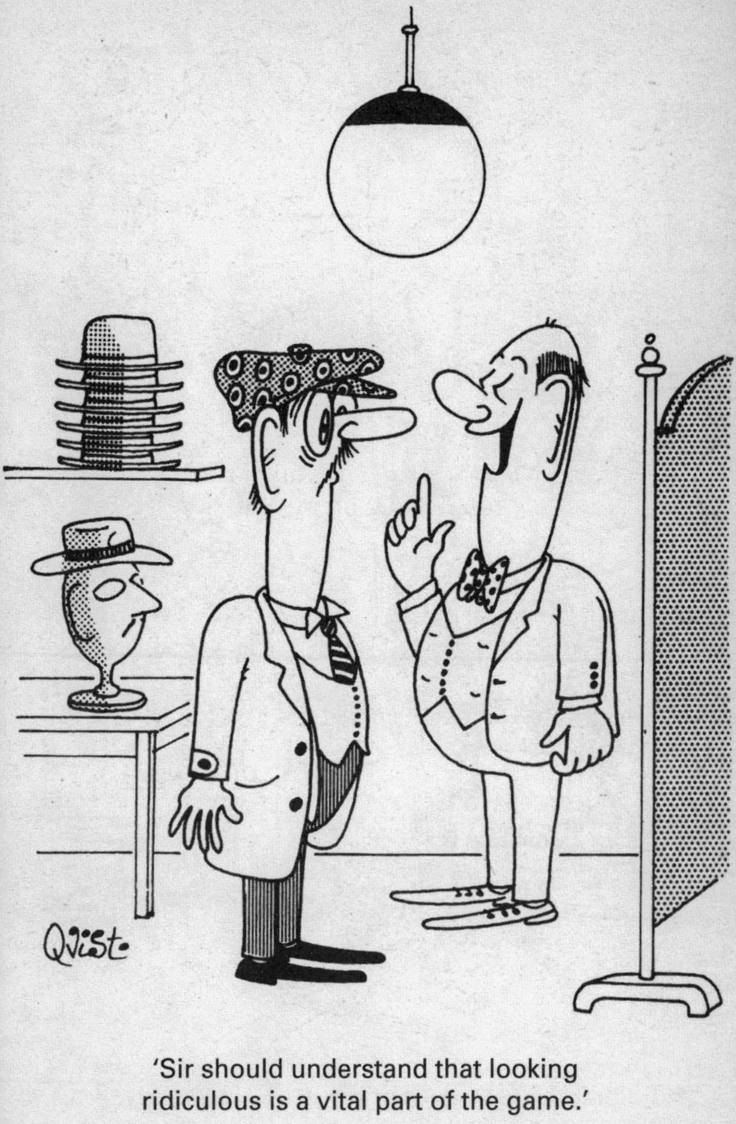
QUIST

'Sir should understand that looking ridiculous is a vital part of the game.'

'You didn't think a wedding would take all day, did you?'

'Well, my initial diagnosis is that
you chose the wrong golfing partner.'

'Too bad our marriage had to end this way, Cora.'

'You're looking tired, Mr Jones – why not go home early and forget about work for the day?'

'Really! There are times when I think
you go and get these chills on purpose.'

'On the other hand, Arnold says here
in the seventh chapter, paragraph fourteen . . .'

'Why sure, darling, you just pop into the club-house
and have a drink. It's your wedding, too.'

'We can't go on meeting like this, love.'

'Take two aspirins, Mrs Jenkins, and call me again in a couple of hours if that hasn't helped.'

'Should that be taken as a hint that you want more democracy in this office, Smith?'

'This happens every time I get
a putter into my hands, doctor.'

'And you have a superb golf course right next door!'

'Your first hole-in-one, I presume?'

'Of course this is the happiest day of my life,
darling. I could never afford a caddie before.'

'Spending the past ten years here correcting
your slice hardly qualifies you for parole.'

'Well, he can't afford polo and he
hasn't really got the time for golf.'

'He can never make up his mind which club to use.'

'They don't seem to be all that advanced.
They just go around hitting small, white balls
with some strange kind of sticks . . .'

'And finally, when you've perfected
your drive, you run out of balls.'

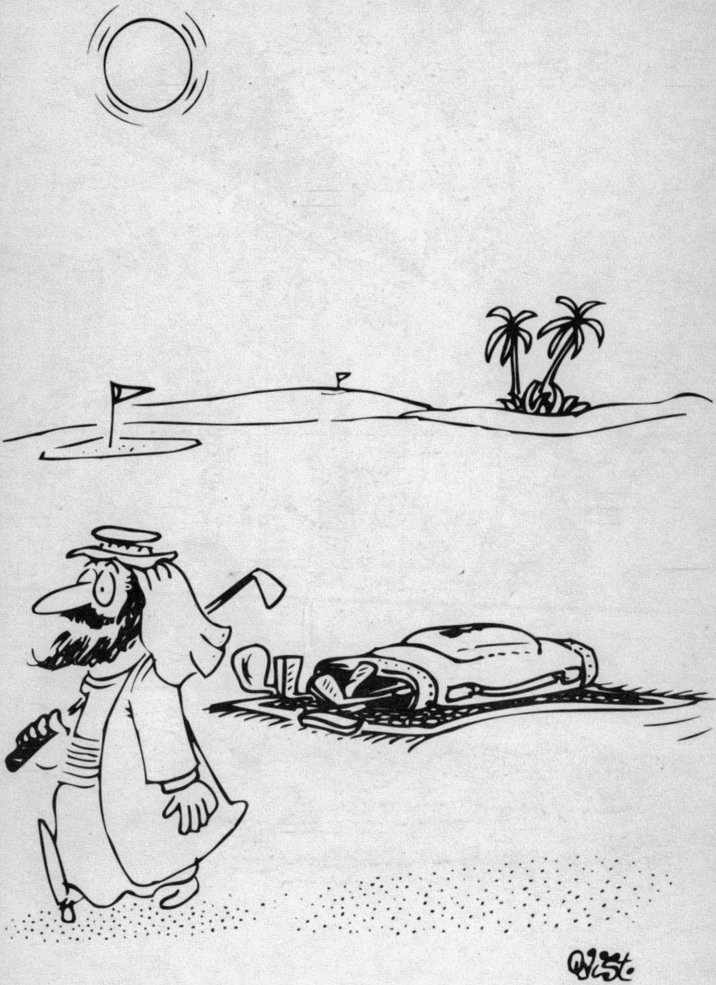

'Not today, I'm afraid – how about
a really early start tomorrow instead?'

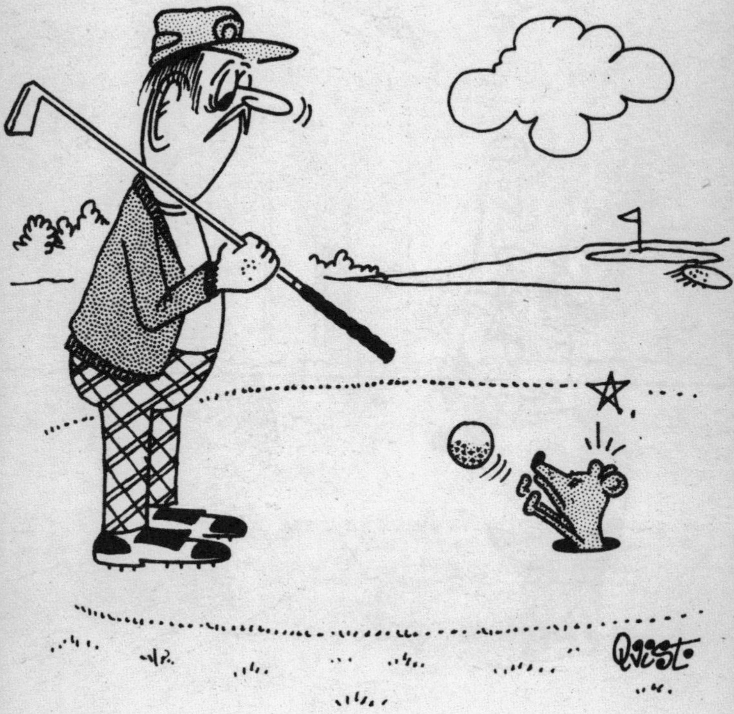
Qvist

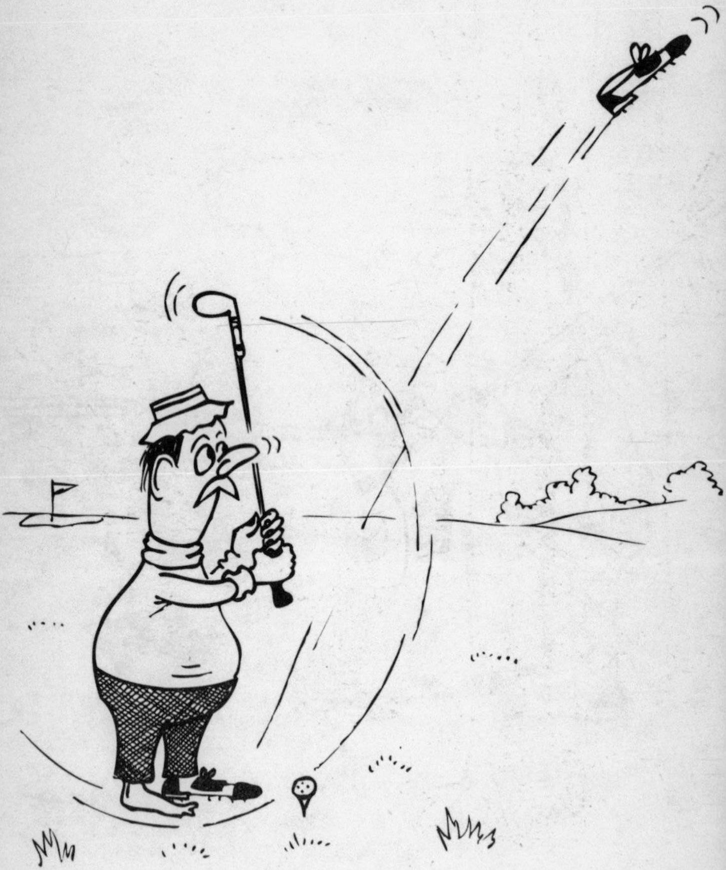

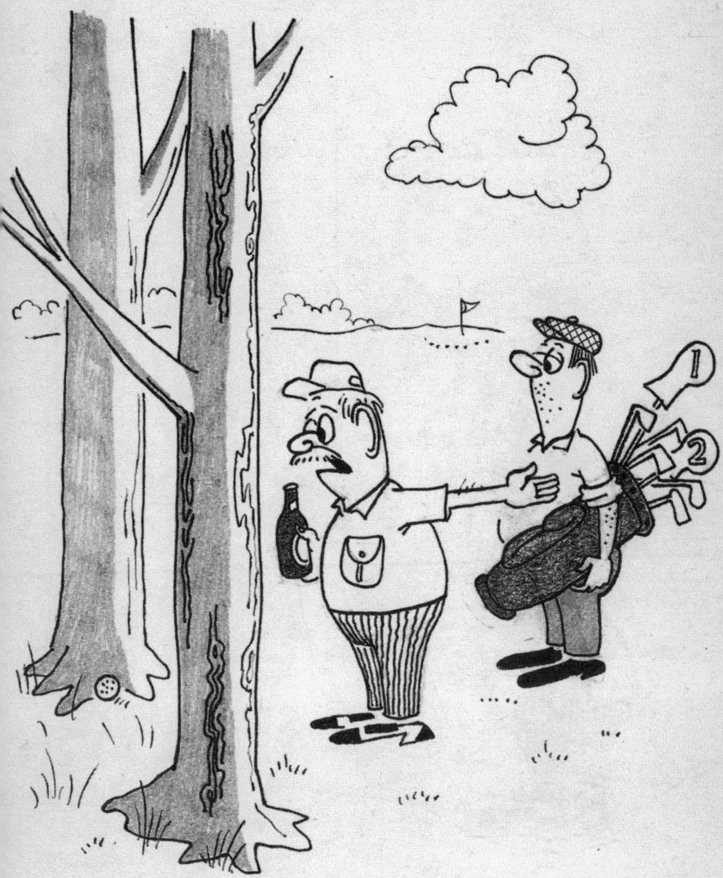
1
2

'Opener, please.'

'Well, she wasn't that keen on it,
but at long last she said I could go.'

OTHER TITLES AVAILABLE IN THIS SERIES

Motor Mania
Garden Mania
Football Mania
Fishing Mania
Sex Mania

Price £2.50 each

These books are available at your local bookshop or newsagent, or can be ordered direct from the publisher.

Just tick the titles you require and fill in the form below. Prices and availability subject to change without notice.

Ravette Books, PO Box 11, Falmouth, Cornwall, TR10 9EN.

Please send a cheque or postal order for the value of the book, and add the following for postage and packing:

UK including BFPO – £1.00 per order.

OVERSEAS, including EIRE – £2.50 per order.

OR Please debit this amount from my Access/Visa Card (delete as appropriate).

CARD NUMBER ☐☐☐☐☐☐☐☐☐☐☐☐☐☐☐☐☐

AMOUNT £............................ EXPIRY DATE ....

SIGNED ....

NAME ....

ADDRESS ....

....

....

....